JESUS 2000

JESUS 2000

The Archbishop of Canterbury's Millennium Message

George Carey

HarperCollins*Publishers*

HarperCollins*Publishers*
77–85 Fulham Palace Road, London W6 8JB

First published in Great Britain in 1999 by
HarperCollins*Publishers*

3 5 7 9 10 8 6 4 2

A catalogue record for this book is available
from the British Library

ISBN 0 551 03220 0

Printed and bound in Great Britain by
Caledonian International Book Manufacturing Ltd, Glasgow

THE ARCHBISHOP OF CANTERBURY'S
MILLENNIUM MESSAGE

ONE SOLITARY LIFE

He was born in an obscure village, the child of a peasant woman. He grew up in another village, where he worked in a carpenter's shop until he was thirty. Then for three years he was an itinerant preacher.

He never wrote a book. He never held office. He never had a family or owned a house. He didn't go to college. He never visited a big city. He never travelled two hundred miles from the place he was born.

He did none of the things one usually associates with greatness. He had no credentials but himself.

He was only thirty-three when the tide of public opinion turned against him. His friends ran away. He was turned over to his enemies and went through the mockery of a trial.

He was nailed to a cross between two thieves. While he was dying, his executioners gambled for his clothing, the only property he had on earth. When he was dead, he was laid in a borrowed grave through the pity of a friend.

Nineteen centuries have come and gone, and today he is the central figure of the human race and the leader of mankind's progress.

All the armies that ever marched, all the navies that ever sailed, all the parliaments that ever sat, all the kings that ever reigned put together, have not affected the life of man on this earth as much as that one solitary life.

It is a curious thing that although we are celebrating the two-thousandth anniversary of the birth of Jesus, many people in western society would admit that they know next to nothing about him. Much of what they do know is dependent on half-forgotten memories of school lessons or Sunday School – and even this may be lacking for many in the younger generation.

Images of Jesus there certainly are. There is the handsome, young, bearded Jesus of old films like *Ben Hur*. There is the 'Che Guevara' figure featured in a recent Church advertising campaign and, of course, there is the familiar Jesus on the cross so central to the devotion of many Christians. But no image can do justice to the person who separates our time into BC (Before Christ) and AD (Anno Domini, 'in the year of our Lord').

This small book is an attempt to bring to life this extraordinary person, who is, in fact, the only reason for these celebrations at all. But why should that attempt be made?

The millennium is all about the opportunities of the future. But it is also a chance to look back. If we look back, we will find that our society and culture are hugely indebted to Jesus and to the meaning he has given to those who have shaped our lives. So if we want to know about our history, we will need to know about Jesus and his impact.

This small book is an attempt to bring to life this extraordinary person, who is, in fact, the only reason for these celebrations at all.

JESUS IS NOT SIMPLY AN HISTORICAL FIGURE

Christians make claims about Jesus which give him potentially far greater significance than anyone else in history. Many reject those claims. But so great are the claims that we should at least know what we are rejecting. A careless dismissal, or simple apathy, cannot form the basis of an alternative creed. We owe it to a faith which has survived 2,000 years – and is wearing well! – to consider these claims thoughtfully.

Some find it impossible to accept these claims, even when they know about them, but it remains true enough to say that those who study this remarkable man come away with their perceptions changed. It is like going on holiday to somewhere you have never been before. If you visit one of the great cities around the world, then in one short holiday you only scratch the surface. There is so much to see. But even if we visit such a place only once, it leaves an indelible mark on us. The millennium is an opportunity to visit the question of Jesus for the first time, or to make a return trip. Everyone should explore this subject at least once in their lives.

Everyone should explore this subject
at least once in their lives.

So far I have been thinking of those who are sceptical or indifferent to the Christian faith. But what of churchgoers themselves? Sadly, I sometimes meet churchgoers whose knowledge of the Founder of their faith is rather shaky. No doubt worship is precious to them, but separated from knowledge of him, their faith will remain unformed and basic. I hope this book will be of some help to them also.

It is worth saying that there is also a rather ironic aspect to this search for Jesus. Look at the world, and most people would agree that great and good things have been done in his name. But the mistakes and failures of Christianity have to be recognized too. I certainly do not want to defend the horrors committed in the name of Jesus. Jesus, of course, is the subject of this book, and he does not excuse them either. If you read the accounts of his life in the Bible you will find no justification for religious wars or discrimination against women. It is an abuse of his life and teaching to drag him into these shameful activities.

That said, there have been great successes as well. Institutions of all kinds – hospitals, schools, universities and orphanages – speak of his continuing impact on our lives. In his name men and women of every age and race have preached his gospel and died for his cause. Many have lived heroic lives and have left behind them works of immense social value.

If the claims made for Jesus and the things he said and did are, to speak candidly, untrue, then all these good and noble things are based on a mistake. All these people have committed themselves and dedicated themselves in vain. That, in itself, should make us look at the alternative interpretation: that behind the noble and good things done in the name of Christ is an amazing person who can inspire us today.

I know what some of you will be thinking: *How can we rely on the Archbishop of Canterbury to be a reliable and objective guide in this search for Jesus of Nazareth?* Surely George Carey will be as unbiased on this subject as, say, Lennox Lewis would be on 'The Art of Boxing' or Steven Spielberg on 'The Benefits of Going to the Cinema'?

How can we rely on the Archbishop of Canterbury to be a reliable and objective guide in this search for Jesus of Nazareth?

There is some truth in that. I acknowledge from the start that I am biased in favour of Jesus. If that puts you off, I am truly sorry; but before you put the book down, let me offer a few thoughts in defence.

I said that exploring the subject of Jesus is a bit like visiting a new place while on holiday. It is also like looking at a great work of art. In a sense, Jesus himself is the author of that work, and as with other artists, it is difficult to write a book about him without seeing some value in what he stood for. Even if you find the Church irritating and a lot of what Jesus taught impractical, you cannot deny the attraction Jesus has for so many. To write a truly unbiased book about Jesus, one would have to be completely indifferent to him. But it would be like someone writing a book about Mozart who thought his music was a series of irritating noises: hardly worthy of anyone's attention.

Even if you find the Church irritating you cannot deny the attraction Jesus has for so many.

Subjectivity is involved in all analysis of movements or ideas. That is a clear and established conclusion in the study of history. Our own subjectivity and experiences inevitably colour our interpretation of facts – even if we have witnessed at first hand the events we describe. The best we can do is try, in all honesty, to keep our bias to a minimum.

In that spirit of absolute honesty, let me make one further comment. The faith I have has been greatly tested and sorely won over many years. It has brought me great blessing, but it has never – I repeat, never – been easy. Like many people, I find that doubt comes readily. I am more predisposed to question than to accept. I was not brought up in the sort of churchgoing home which gives a young person's faith security and strength. The faith I have has been earned through much questioning, through doubt and struggle, and through life's experiences of good and ill. Through all these struggles my understanding of the person of Jesus Christ has grown, has deepened, has been refined and absorbed. I believe I can be a true and loyal guide to the honest questioners, because I know exactly how they feel. So I hope you will persevere, and find in me an honest guide to the reason for the millennium celebrations: this amazing person, Jesus.

The faith I have has brought me great blessing,
but it has never – I repeat, never – been easy.

At the beginning of this century, that simple question was very much in dispute. Some German academics claimed that Jesus was simply a figment of the imagination. The writers of the New Testament, they said, had fabricated the story of this 'Christ', in order to found a new faith in the credulous world of the Roman Empire. Few, if any, contemporary experts take that view now, for three basic reasons.

Firstly, even if we believe the stories of Jesus Christ (called the Gospels) to be written as late as 40 years after Jesus' death, that is still 'within living memory'. Some people would still have been alive who could testify against the Gospels as a fabrication; who would remember nothing about a crucifixion at Passover-time in Jerusalem. No group of writers could have succeeded with such a fabrication. Indeed, the letters of Paul, which were written far earlier, witness against the charge that the person of Jesus is just a myth.

Some people would still have been alive who could testify against the Gospels as a fabrication.

Secondly, there is no evidence of collective fabrication among the different writers of the New Testament. True, there are many similarities in the accounts. But given the difficulties in communication at this time, it is hard to see, practically, how the

Gospel writers who recorded the life of Jesus could have co-operated to make up such a story. There are very extensive differences as well. Surely that means that there was no connivance or fabrication. The idea, then, that Jesus was 'faked' is extremely implausible.

The idea that Jesus was 'faked' is extremely implausible.

Thirdly, non-Christian sources of the time were clearly aware of a person who was the founder of the Christian sect. Writing about the persecution of Christians in the year AD 64, Tacitus comments that the name 'Christians' comes 'from Christ, who was condemned to death during the reign of Tiberius by the procurator Pontius Pilate'. Pliny the Younger, Suetonius and Josephus, a Jewish historian, also refer to the existence of Jesus, called the Christ.

It is my conclusion that we may affirm, with confidence, that a man of flesh and blood stands behind the documents which speak of him.

CAN WE TRUST THE NEW TESTAMENT?

Experts now agree that the earliest writings are not the Gospels but the letters of Paul, written some 20 years after the death and resurrection of Jesus. The earliest Gospel, Mark, was probably written about 30 years after his death. Although the Gospels have much in common with each other, they do have significant differences as well.

On the basis of the time-gap and the differences, we could recoil into scepticism and say, 'All right, we believe Jesus existed, but how can we trust the New Testament to tell us anything reliable about him?'

Such scepticism is not warranted. We are forgetting the impact Jesus made on the people of his day. If Jesus was great enough to die for – and we have independent historical evidence that Christians were dying in his cause before the first Gospel is supposed to have been written – it would have been a natural instinct to preserve the stories of his life and teaching.

If Jesus was great enough to die for, it would have been a natural instinct to preserve the stories of his life and teaching.

We must remember the importance of an 'oral tradition' to people of Jesus' own time and, indeed, for people of the Middle East up to the present day. The word 'tradition' seems to us to imply something unreliable and uncertain, but this is not how *they* would understand it. For them, remembering and constantly repeating stories and sayings was the only way of keeping alive the teaching of their Rabbi. Faithfulness in doing so was essential. What is more, the 'remembering' was more than the responsibility of the individual: the community or the family remembered together and the faithful handing on of the tradition was crucially important. For the first followers of Jesus Christ, the task would have been made easier by the colourful and entertaining quality of his teaching. His parables and stories were powerful, relevant and memorable. So before the documents were ever written down, there would have been a reliable tradition behind them.

It is much the same with war memories today. History books are still being written now about the events of the Gulf War, the Falklands War, the Vietnam War and the Second World War. The recollections of those who fought in the battles are used on TV documentaries to record what actually happened. The Second World War happened over 50 years ago, but we still trust the accounts of the people who took part in it.

Reading the New Testament is not a simple matter. Unlike a straightforward modern history book, there are many ways of understanding what the New Testament says. But if we accept it as the most complete source of information we have about Jesus, and read it with care, then we have an astonishingly rich seam to mine. Once we have understood that these are not modern documents – even though they are as complex and subtle as many a modern work – then we can trust them to yield more than just information.

WHAT KIND OF PERSON WAS JESUS?

So at last we come to the New Testament and begin our search. Our first question will probably be: 'What kind of man was he?' Answering this question illustrates perfectly what I have just said about the nature of the New Testament, for we meet a surprising problem here.

If you and I were writing a story about Jesus today, we would describe his appearance, clothes, mannerisms and habits; we would discuss his interests, relationships and talents; we would outline in great detail the arguments he had with his adversaries, and we would analyse his unusual teaching. But the New Testament is not very interested in these details. We ask, 'What is there for us to *know*?' The New Testament asks, 'What is there to be *believed*?'

That is precisely what the New Testament sets before us: a person who came with a message to be believed. Jesus' question to the disciples, 'Who do you say I am?' is a question he addresses to everyone.

> *Jesus' question to the disciples, 'Who do you say I am?' is a question he addresses to everyone.*

When Peter tried to answer that disconcerting question, he did not say, 'You are a young Jew from Nazareth.' He talked, rather, about Jesus' significance. He said, 'You are the Messiah, the Son of God.' We too must concern ourselves primarily with Jesus' significance.

Yet a real person *is* discernible in the Gospel accounts. Jesus was a Jew and was rooted in the Jewish culture of his time. He knew family life, lived in a small town – Nazareth – with his parents – Joseph and Mary – and his brothers and sisters. He would have been apprenticed to his father, possibly as a carpenter. And while the Gospels do not set out to give us a physical description of Jesus, they allow us tantalizing glimpses of his humanity. He knew what it was to work to the point of exhaustion, what it was to be hungry and what it was to love, to feel anger, grief, loneliness and fear. Though we have no reports of him laughing, his teaching shows that he had a sense of humour. Though he never went to a place of higher learning, he grew in knowledge and, later in life, was seen to have the authority of a Rabbi (a religious teacher). His teaching reveals a canny knowledge of human beings, and a love of nature and the countryside.

Although no description comes down to us through the centuries, there is no doubt that he was a riveting public personality, arresting, allusive and provocative. All four accounts of his life speak of the huge crowds that followed him. They hung on every word as he spoke in parables about everyday life, about the nature of God and his kingdom, and about religious duties. And he inspired strong emotions: people were passionately for or against him.

They hung on every word as he spoke in parables about everyday life.

Here we come to the *controversial* nature of this curious person, Jesus. The picture from our Sunday School lessons of 'gentle Jesus, meek and mild' bears little resemblance to the real man. He was not the caricature that the novelist Nabokov describes as 'a blond-bearded faddist in a towelling robe'. He was a man who roused anger and deep controversy with the people in authority in his day. He got dirt under his fingernails. He was prepared to confront the religious establishment of the time and speak of the priests as 'hypocrites' who did not practise what they preached. In the eyes of some, his attack on the money-lenders in the temple was a shocking attack on religious authority in general. All four Gospel accounts describe this extraordinary and bold action, and each one records that the outraged leaders asked, 'By what authority are you doing these things and who gave you that authority?'

He was prepared to confront the religious establishment of the time and speak of the priests as 'hypocrites' who did not practise what they preached.

We need to think about this word 'authority'. With it we are at the centre of understanding the man called Jesus of Nazareth. We all know controversial figures today; and we know what happens when the label 'controversial' is attached to them. Their power to shock and surprise us is at once diminished. We respond to the latest outburst with, 'Well, he would say that, wouldn't he?' Controversy simply makes them look contrary.

That could have happened to Jesus. He could have been just

another 'holy fool', outrageous, but ultimately ignored. That was the fate of many preachers – so why not Jesus? The answer is to do with the authority his contemporaries clearly understood that he had.

BY WHOSE AUTHORITY DID JESUS ACT AND SPEAK?

As Jesus went about his work as a healer, preacher and leader, something very interesting became obvious to his hearers and followers. Not only did he talk about God with great eloquence and insight, but he claimed the authority of God for what he did. He did not rely on the backing of Rabbinical scholarship to defend his teaching. He spoke directly, even contradicting teaching from the past. And his claims were backed up by what happened. The evidence of remarkable healings and the way he took on the authorities of his day spoke of an extraordinary relationship with God. He had an instinctive grasp of what was good and holy, a clear sense of what was God's will. There was also the evidence of the way he lived. He did not work from the comfort and security of a university study or a church office but in the context of ordinary life. He actually led the life he called others to follow.

His claims were backed up by what happened.

If we were to explore in depth what kind of man Jesus was, this sense of authority would be our most striking find. It was certainly so for those first 'explorers', his disciples. And it would remain so for centuries to come, in his Church.

Despite this authority, Jesus provoked great animosity, and ultimately suffered a cruel and untimely death. Still a young man (about 33), he was executed in public, reviled by the mob, with very few friends in sight. What made him so many enemies? To answer this question we need to look at exactly what Jesus taught.

UNDERSTANDING THE KINGDOM OF GOD

Facing the early years of the new millennium, many of us are looking to make a fresh start in a 'new' world. Every generation tries to do this. But we have a helpful chronological illustration for what we are trying to do: the year 2000 really feels like something different, a new page in history. Jesus also spoke of a 'new world'. He called it 'the kingdom'.

This was the burden of his parables and the meaning behind his entire life. In Mark's Gospel Jesus' first words are: 'The time has come. The kingdom of God is upon you; repent and believe the good news.' These words explain the whole life and work of Jesus. This is a new world because it is ruled by God, in justice and peace. 'God's moment in history has dawned – God's good news is now available; turn around and receive it.'

Jesus certainly did not mean a kingdom as we would understand it. In fact, while using the term, he turned the whole notion of 'kingdom' on its head. This was no hierarchical state with a glittering monarch at its head and a mass of poor, downtrodden subjects. It was not even to be thought of as a territory – like the

United Kingdom or the Kingdom of Oman. For Jesus the word described the rule of God over the hearts of people. This rule was not a tyrannical grip: being accepted into the kingdom involved a free and loving response to God. Everyone is able to make such a response, so the kingdom is open to everyone, irrespective of their position in the kingdoms of the world. This *freedom* is a crucial element of Jesus' teaching.

The kingdom is open to everyone, irrespective of their position in the kingdoms of the world.

Jesus, of course, was a Jew. The Jewish Law (the Torah) was important to him and he sought to obey it. There were, however, some 613 laws to know and follow and the burden of them was often very hard for ordinary people. Later in his ministry Jesus attacked the religious law-makers: 'They tie up heavy loads and put them on people's shoulders, but they themselves are not willing to lift a finger to move them.' Laws and regulations remain a problematic feature of all religions today. For Christianity, one problem is that law can stand in the way of God's unconditional love, as revealed in Jesus. Instead of being a door through which we go to be closer to God, law becomes a barrier.

THE GREATEST COMMANDMENT

If you read about Jesus in the Gospels, you will notice that legalism is completely missing in Jesus' teaching about the kingdom. There is no neat set of rules which the believer must obey, step by step, to obtain salvation. Jesus says, 'Repent and believe the gospel, the good news,' and he reduces the complex system of Jewish laws to two: love God with your whole being, and love your neighbour as much as you love yourself. These are commandments which every member of the human race can aim to keep, despite differences of culture, ability and belief. Anyone who sees God as some kind of divine policeman out to spoil everyone's fun has missed the point. The Bible reveals a God of love.

What Jesus said had radical implications for his society. He spoke of 'proclaiming freedom for the captives' and 'recovery of sight for the blind', 'release for the oppressed' and 'the jubilee'. And just as there is this liberation from the law in Jesus' teaching, it is also there in his actions. We find him mingling with tax collectors and sinners, prostitutes and lepers, the very poor and even Samaritans and non-Jews, all of whom were 'beyond the pale' to respectable, law-keeping Jews of the day. He was a man of the people whose whole ministry was slanted towards the disadvantaged. His compassion was tangible, and he spoke in tones of tenderness to those in distress. He did not rebuke those whose lives were in a mess, but reserved his anger for those who caused God's 'little ones' to stumble. His compassion for those who were lost and bewildered comes across in his parables and through his actions.

What Jesus said had radical implications for his society.

The main characteristic of his lifestyle was his extraordinary generosity – in being prepared to forgive harm done and not strike back, in making those on the boundaries of society feel accepted, and in being prepared to give up everything for the cause of the kingdom. Where the Church has not portrayed this Jesus, we have failed both him and you. Jesus saw his whole life as an offering to others. To be open to the wonder of grace in people's lives is to take risks, and to stake everything on a change. Jesus did just that. Those who search for the kingdom, he said, will find it – but you must be like a merchant who, when he has found the precious pearl he has been looking for, sells everything in order to possess it. By losing everything, we gain everything and are truly set free.

HOW WOULD THIS FREEDOM COME ABOUT?

Jesus probably believed that God's kingdom would one day extend over all people, but in the Gospels, the focus is initially on the kingdom taking hold of us here and now. And not with sudden drama and grandeur, as a heavenly *coup d'etat*. In the parables of Jesus there is a striking emphasis on 'smallness' and 'insignificance'.

The focus is on the kingdom taking hold of us here and now.

17

For example, Jesus told a story about a mustard seed. It was supposed to be Palestine's smallest seed, and was thus proverbial for the least significant of all things. But from it grows a tree, and the birds of the air shelter in its branches. There is space for everyone in the kingdom of God, from the greatest to the least; from royalty and celebrities to the most ordinary person on the street.

Another illustration he used was of yeast in dough: a little leaven can make a loaf for many hungry people. God's rule is like that, said Jesus. 'Let him take over and he can transform the most hopeless matter – it has the potential to grow into something quite amazing.' No kingdom has such a caring monarch. But that is the point about the kingdom of God. As someone once remarked to me, the curious thing about the kingdom as Jesus saw it was that 'there is no King – only a Father'.

ALL ABOUT PRAYER

This leads us to the prayer which Jesus taught his followers: that incomparable gift to us all, *the 'Lord's Prayer'*.

> *Our Father, which art in heaven,*
> *Hallowed be thy Name.*
> *Thy kingdom come.*
> *Thy will be done,*
> *in earth as it is in heaven.*
> *Give us this day our daily bread.*

And forgive us our trespasses,
As we forgive them that trespass against us.
And lead us not into temptation;
But deliver us from evil.

In the English version of Matthew's Gospel, the Lord's Prayer is just 55 words long! Fifty-five precious words which have sustained millions of people in all human circumstances – war and peace, famine and plenty, tragedy and celebration.

It was used at one particular time of sadness which I shall never forget: the funeral of Diana, Princess of Wales in Westminster Abbey, on 2 September 1997. It fell to me to conduct the prayers and so to lead everyone in the Lord's Prayer. I was told later that possibly 2.4 billion people watched the BBC service and there is no doubt that this was the largest number of people ever to say that beloved prayer together. People throughout the world instinctively knew, without any embarrassment, that these were the right words to say when all other words failed. I received many letters which said something like: 'That was the moment when I felt we were entrusting Princess Diana to a Heavenly Father.' A remarkable thing about the Lord's Prayer is that it is not just for Christians. Jews, Muslims and people of a number of other faiths have told me they can say it wholeheartedly. The funeral of Diana, Princess of Wales showed that this is literally, as one theologian put it, 'the prayer that spans the world'.

The Lord's Prayer tells us what God is like.

The Lord's Prayer is very much a teaching prayer. The disciples, Luke tells us, asked Jesus: 'Lord, teach us to pray.' Jesus did not give them a lecture, he taught them this prayer: 'When you pray, say Our Father...'. As well as putting into words our human concerns ('Give us this day our daily bread'), it also tells us a lot about our relationship with God. 'Father' is the important word here. Of course, this does not mean simple masculinity – it is a word picture of God's *character*. If we had asked Jesus, 'What is God like?' the answer would have been, 'He is like a parent, a Father who cares for us and whom we can trust.' Moving on to say 'who art in heaven', we find that although God is 'Our Father', we can know him in a way that transcends all human relationships.

The rest of the prayer is really a development of our trust in God. His name should be 'respected and loved', we should pray for the coming of God's kingdom in the hearts of all, and we should accept God's will. We should look to him to provide for our daily nourishment. We should give thanks for the knowledge that we are forgiven, and ask for grace to forgive the sins of others and be led away from the temptation to sin. Finally, we should acknowledge that the kingdom – the subject of the prayer – is God's everlasting kingdom.

The prayer is really a development of our trust in God.

Let me share with you a particular sadness I feel today: about our ignorance of the Lord's Prayer. When parents and schools fail to put this prayer at the centre of a child's life, they are depriving him or

20

her of a commodity which has become very rare – *hope*. The Lord's Prayer has been a source of faith and hope for generations of people, regardless of the actual strength of their faith. It has a power to sustain and support people in the bleak moments of life. It can set the seal on the good times.

Why is this so? I have not yet explained that the Aramaic word for 'Father' is *Abba* – a child's word for 'Daddy'. It is the language of trust. We are all familiar with the advantages children have when they enjoy the support and security of a good parent. If children grow up with an awareness that they have a heavenly parent as well, that belief has the capacity to transform their lives. The stability, the faith and the encouragement to hope which the Lord's Prayer gives to a person can be transmitted into all areas of that person's life, from beginning to end. Just 52 words. To teach your children this prayer will be a legacy of faith, hope and love beyond price. The Lord's Prayer assures us all that in this hard, often cruel world, there is a God who loves us and by whom we are accepted.

The Aramaic word for 'Father' is Abba –
a child's word for 'Daddy'.

While some people prefer the traditional words of the Lord's Prayer given earlier, here is a more modern version that you might like to use instead.

> *Our Father in heaven,*
> *hallowed be your name,*
> *your kingdom come,*
> *your will be done,*
> *on earth as in heaven.*
> *Give us today our daily bread.*
> *Forgive us our sins*
> *as we forgive those who sin against us.*
> *Lead us not into temptation*
> *but deliver us from evil.*

GOD'S MANIFESTO

If the Lord's Prayer is the prayer of the kingdom of God, then the *Sermon on the Mount* is its manifesto, proclaiming its ideals and values.

If you go to the Holy Land today you will probably visit the octagonal church built on what is called the 'Mount of Beatitudes' overlooking the sea of Galilee. The octagonal shape commemorates the eight 'beatitudes' (blessings) which come at the beginning of the sermon, found in the fifth chapter of Matthew's Gospel. This sermon is a sort of summary of Jesus' teaching, probably emphasized many times throughout his career. Matthew brought it all together to give to the Church a powerful outline of Jesus' teaching on kingdom 'ethics', or the way to live.

What was this radical teaching? Although the 'sermon' is relatively short, it has prompted reams of analysis over the centuries. We cannot go into the arguments in any detail here, but let's look at the heart of what Jesus said.

Blessed are the poor in spirit, for theirs is the kingdom of heaven.
Blessed are those who mourn, for they will be comforted.
Blessed are the meek, for they will inherit the earth.
Blessed are those who hunger and thirst for righteousness, for they will be filled.
Blessed are the merciful, for they will receive mercy.
Blessed are the pure in heart, for they will see God.
Blessed are the peacemakers, for they will be called children of God.
Blessed are those who are persecuted for righteousness' sake, for theirs is the kingdom of heaven.

These are the 'blessed sayings'. In eight terse sentences Jesus describes the kind of people who are blessed and will be blessed by God. Which people in the world count as fortunate and blessed? Well, we know the answers – the wealthy, the famous, the successful and the gifted. Jesus rejects this definition. It is actually the poor; those in need both of human help and God's help; those who long to see justice prevail; those who mourn; the compassionate; the peacemakers; the pure hearted; and those who are prepared to face persecution for the sake of what is right. Again, we can note the contrary character of the kingdom. Jesus' 'topsy-turvy' approach would have seemed as extraordinary in his day as it does in ours. Jesus says, 'These people are the salt that keeps society from going rotten and the light to illuminate a dark world.'

Which people in the world count as fortunate?
The wealthy, the famous, the successful and the gifted.
Jesus rejects this definition.

Of course, in talking about this unconventional kingdom, Jesus had to challenge the conventions of his day. This meant a challenge to the way God's Law in the Hebrew Scriptures was being interpreted. Though many have seen Jesus' teaching as an outright attack on contemporary Judaism, in fact he was simply trying to change its focus. He wanted to apply the Law to people's hearts, not just to their external behaviour.

Here are some examples of what Jesus taught:

- 'The Law said, "No murder." I say, "Even the hatred that can lead to murder is wrong." '
- 'The Law said, "No adultery." I say, "Don't even commit it by lusting after someone in your heart." '
- 'The Law said, "You can get a divorce with a certificate of dismissal." I say, "Divorce is far more serious than that." '
- 'The Law said, "Don't swear falsely." I say, "Don't swear at all." '
- 'The Law said, "An eye for an eye." I say, "No vengeance whatsoever." '
- 'The Law said, "Love your neighbour." I say, "Love your enemy." '

We must always remember that Jesus sought to break down anything that came between the loving God and his needy creation. He passionately wants to have a personal relationship with each one of us. Not for him the bland religious discourse which ends so often in doing nothing and changing no one. He spoke bluntly and not, perhaps, without humour. 'If someone strikes you on the right cheek, offer the left!' 'If someone forces you to go one mile, go with him two!' 'If someone takes your coat, give him your cloak as well!' 'If your eye causes you to sin, pluck it out!'

He spoke bluntly and not, perhaps, without humour.

Vivid, direct and colourful. But is it *practical*?

HOW ARE WE TO INTERPRET THE SAYINGS IN THE SERMON ON THE MOUNT?

Jesus' teaching is usually very relevant and grounded in what people experience – the parables are tales of everyday life. But the teaching in these sayings from the Sermon on the Mount seems impossibly idealistic. How could anyone follow or obey these almost inhuman commands?

Once again, we have to look at it from the perspective of the kingdom. Jesus was not bringing in a new law for sinless people, but was giving an outline of the kind of behaviour expected of those who are being called into the kingdom of God. In short, Jesus was saying to people: 'If you follow me, then here is a vision of the life you are called to follow. You won't always achieve it, but it's a standard that will inspire and attract you.' It still does.

UNDERSTANDING MIRACLES

Jesus was known as a teacher – but he was also famous as a healer and a worker of what we have come to call 'miracles'. Perhaps, as you read this, some of you are groaning with impatience. 'Now come on, surely no one believes in miracles these days! Even some of your bishops and clergy admit that it's unlikely they happened!'

If we place any value at all on the Bible as a record of what Jesus said and did, the importance of the 'miraculous' in his life and work is a fact. But that fact is a great embarrassment to some people, and many have tried to get around it.

It used to be argued that details of miracles were later additions to the story of Jesus when the cult around him grew. There is no evidence for that, however, and biblical experts now accept that 'signs and wonders' were part of the story of Jesus from the beginning. Even pagan sources spoke of Jesus as someone who 'went around doing good and healing the people'. One-third of the entire Gospel of Mark, the earliest to be written, is composed of stories which describe Jesus' miraculous power over nature and people.

Even pagan sources spoke of Jesus as someone who 'went around doing good and healing the people'.

Of course, if we are convinced today that the miraculous is just impossible, then we have a problem with Jesus. And it is *our* problem because, as I have said, there is no escaping the centrality of 'mighty works' in his life. There are two things we might consider, to quell our natural scepticism.

Firstly, I suggest that our problem with the miracles of Jesus might, like our problem with the image of Jesus, stem from a caricature. Just as we might misrepresent Jesus as 'meek and mild' on the basis of a selective view of him, we might also believe the miracles to be incredible because we look at only a few of them. Certainly, there are those 'wonders' which are an instant affront to our understanding of nature: a man walks on water and calms a storm, for example. How can this be? For Jesus' original audience, it was just as amazing for him to say 'love your enemies' or to consort with lepers as it was for him to feed the five thousand. We may find it difficult to believe some of the miraculous things which he is said to have done, but we cannot afford to ignore just how different his life and teachings were from those of his contemporaries. Both provoked awe and wonder amongst those who knew him.

For Jesus' original audience, it was just as amazing for him to say 'love your enemies' or to consort with lepers as it was for him to feed the five thousand.

Secondly, although the idea that miracles happen is a problem for the modern mind, we might also acknowledge that life itself is extraordinarily 'miraculous'. For instance, we are reliably informed that the whole of intelligent life was encoded in the first three seconds of the creation of the universe following the 'Big Bang'. If that is not something to wonder at, then we have lost our capacity to wonder.

But let us return to the 'wonder' implicit in the ministry of Jesus. The words chosen in Matthew, Mark and Luke to describe his remarkable power are 'mighty works', whereas John's account of his life uses the word 'signs'. The interesting point about the miracles of Jesus is that they were never done to *prove* that he was God's son. Many other prophets of the time performed miracles. But according to Mark, Jesus hushed it all up and commanded people not to tell others. 'There shall no signs be given to this generation,' he said.

WHY DID JESUS DO 'MIGHTY WORKS'?

The answer to this question is that miracles were, for Jesus, *signs of the kingdom*. If the kingdom meant the sovereign action of God, then the 'works' were 'mighty' because they signalled the activity of God. They told the 'good news' that the kingdom had arrived in the person of Jesus. They demonstrated that feature of the kingdom which I wrote about earlier, for these miracles showed life turned upside-down, confounding our expectations.

While we recognize the miraculous element in the ministry of Jesus, we must not exaggerate it. It is not the main element in his life. For example, in the Gospel of Mark, 'mighty works' are prominent in the first part of the book, but as Jesus' attention swings to his approaching visit to Jerusalem and his death, so miracles recede into the background. At the very climax of the story, the 'mighty' Jesus becomes the crucified Jesus, deserted by his friends and handed over to death.

*While we recognize the miraculous
element in the ministry of Jesus,
we must not exaggerate it.*

Ultimately, any questions we might have about the miracles must come second to our estimate of Jesus himself. If he was only a 'good man' with all the adjectives we might wish to attribute to him – holy, charismatic, and so on – then we shall wish to discard the miracle stories as legends ascribed by others. If, on the other hand, we get to the point of believing with the first disciples that through this man, Jesus, God has revealed himself, we might reasonably accept that there is nothing surprising whatever about the creator of the universe giving his son power over sin, disease and death.

Perhaps we need to reserve judgement for the moment, and learn more about the man behind the millennium, the reason why we are celebrating the year 2000.

DEATH: THE FINAL AND GREATEST MYSTERY

We have looked at the facts about Jesus: the fact that he actually existed, that he commanded authority, that he taught a very daring message, that the miraculous was part of his story. These are all facts which, we might say, have little to do with us directly. They need not affect us at all. However, the most important fact of all about

Jesus converges with the most important fact of all about each one of us: death. For each of us, the fact of death will end our lives, and we shape our lives according to that fact. But the fact of death did *not* finish Jesus' life, and that, surely, must interest all of us.

The most important fact of all about Jesus converges with the most important fact of all about each one of us: death.

Before we look at his death, though, there is a problem we must address. The four accounts of Jesus' life in the Bible were, as I have said, written by followers of Jesus after his death and resurrection. They believed in him and wanted others to become followers too. So the Gospels are confessional documents – tracts written to convince people that Jesus is the Christ. There are those who believe that the first writers coloured their accounts with the view that Jesus was God, and therefore the Gospels are unlikely to give us a true record of the reasons for Jesus' death.

There are those who believe that the first writers coloured their accounts with the view that Jesus was God.

Such scepticism is understandable but unnecessary. Imagine if he was *just* an unusual man with great gifts of eloquence and charisma

– and that some followers later tried to promote him into the leader of a new sect. If that were the case, we might retort, there was already something pretty marvellous in the story of Jesus to warrant such adoration and special treatment! There had been many great leaders – charismatic, eloquent and intelligent teachers – in that tumultuous century, but only Jesus of Nazareth gets this kind of treatment. Why?

For myself, I have no reason to doubt that the story of Jesus' growing conflict with the authorities of his day is correct and points to the threat they perceived him to be. The Gospels report that from the beginning of Jesus' public life he was regarded as a controversial figure; a serious challenge, in fact, to the religious establishment of his time.

Jesus was regarded as a controversial figure; a serious challenge, in fact, to the religious establishment of his time.

All four accounts in the Bible report that the turning point in Jesus' life was his decision to go up to Jerusalem to celebrate the annual Passover festival. He had, the writers tell us, already dropped several hints that things could turn out badly. He amazed his disciples as he spoke darkly of his impending death, which he treated in terms of 'sacrifice'. His teaching contained clues that he saw himself as a 'Messiah' bound for death; a leader who was willing to die for his people, and who saw that death as his destiny.

We must therefore reject the idea that here was a confused but holy and good man wandering up to Jerusalem with the noble intention of simply joining in an annual religious festival. Besides, the Passover-time when Jesus was on his final journey was far more than just another religious festival. It commemorated the liberation of the Israelites from the power of the Egyptians centuries earlier. Given that the Israelites were again oppressed by a foreign power – this time the Romans – it was a natural focus for the aspirations and longings of the people. Throughout Jesus' adult life, the feast of the Passover would have had nationalist and military overtones, as a symbol of the overthrow of power. For someone who had famously championed the cause of the victim and the oppressed, the road to Jerusalem was a dangerous one to take.

More dangerous still, Jesus' teaching about the kingdom shared much with the teaching of his revolutionary contemporaries, and in his encounters with the authorities in that last week of his life, this 'kingdom' was an implicit theme. It would have been very easy for the authorities to make the mistake which we guarded against earlier on, and believe the kingdom to be a rival state bent on overthrowing the present regime. But Jesus cleverly played down the nationalist overtones of his teaching by making his crucial entry into Jerusalem on a donkey. He had no intention of being killed on the outskirts of Jerusalem by troops sent to crush a riot: he was aiming for the heart of the capital. All this preparation suggests that he was not just a good leader in the wrong place at the wrong time. He had deliberately chosen to be there – to take away the sin of the world.

He was not just a good leader in the wrong place
at the wrong time. He had deliberately chosen
to be there – to take away the sin of the world.

WHY DID JESUS DIE?

A clue to Jesus' ideas about his own death is given at the famous 'Last Supper'. Once again, it shows that the kingdom of God which Jesus spoke of overturns human expectations. It also shows that Jesus himself was the inauguration of that kingdom.

It was probably a Passover meal, traditional for all Jews, but Jesus gives it a much wider significance. He took the bread, the meal's 'substance', and said, 'This is my body.' The substance of the Passover is no longer the lamb which was slaughtered as a sacrifice under the old laws, but Jesus himself. The wine is taken with the words, 'This is the blood of the covenant which is poured out for many. I shall not drink it again until I drink it anew in the kingdom of God.' This refers to the previous covenant between Israel and God which was confirmed by a sprinkling of blood, again from an animal sacrifice. This time, the blood will be from the sacrifice of Jesus himself.

For me, this is the spiritual centre of the life, death and legacy of Jesus Christ. This is what he was about. He saw, and the later Church realized, that his imminent death would be a sacrifice offered to God for the sins of all people. Scholars disagree about the precise meaning of this sacrifice. But there is a common acceptance that from the earliest times this death was seen as a gift offered for us all to God the Father. It signifies a new covenant – an agreement sealed through blood – that God and humankind are now reconciled. It is now possible to know God personally.

For me, this is the spiritual centre of the life,
death and legacy of Jesus Christ.
This is what he was about.

This meal has been remembered faithfully ever since (in the service of holy communion) as a sacrament, a 'sign' of the new covenant and the new kingdom. I find it nothing less than awesome that there has been an unbroken continuity in the celebration of this sacrament from Christ's day to our own. Somewhere in the world, every week – even today as you read this book – this ritual, inessential for survival, and immaterial to physical satisfaction, has been re-enacted for nearly two millennia. This is surely unique in the history of humankind, and it has only happened because of this man Jesus.

He was taken from that meal to his death.

WHY WAS HE CONDEMNED TO DEATH?

We have already noted that there is a spiritual or theological answer we can readily give to this question. Jesus died for us and our sins. He paid the price for our failings and wickedness, and restored the possibility of union between human beings and their creator. The Church has always declared this truth to be at the heart of the Christian faith.

There is an historical answer we should give as well.

We have seen that Jesus did not avoid controversy – and nor should we today. His teaching was controversial, and he taught controversially. God's kingdom would redress wrongs and vindicate the despised in society. This would never be a popular message, for the wronged and despised were not in the majority. Jesus proclaimed this unpopular message with such boldness and skill that he was greatly resented by those he criticized. Although he was very popular with ordinary people, for the Romans and the Jewish authorities there was little idea of free speech and the right to dissent. Jesus had made too many enemies to last long.

Although he was very popular with ordinary people, Jesus had made too many enemies to last long.

Nevertheless, teaching alone would not have been sufficient for such an extreme act as public crucifixion – unless, in addition, he was guilty of a far more serious crime. Had he claimed in his teaching, either directly or indirectly, to be God's chosen servant, the 'Messiah'? If so, the charge of blasphemy could be brought against him. Others had made similar claims in Jesus' day, but few had been so unorthodox or disruptive in their interpretations of how a Messiah should behave.

I need to say here, as firmly as I can, that the fact that Jesus was crucified by fellow Jews does not condone anti-Semitism in any shape or form. Some sections of the Church in the past have used the crucifixion of Jesus as a reason for persecuting the Jews. The New Testament, taken as a whole, gives us *no* authority to do so. For Christians, Jews have a very special place in God's purposes. Jesus was a Jew and Christians should honour the remarkable debt we owe to Judaism.

But let us return to the accusation against Jesus. The crime Jesus committed was that he refused to be put in a box and labelled as a political extremist, a religious nut or a harmless romantic. Even today he does not match up to the image of a vicar in TV soap operas or comedy programmes. He cannot be 'tidied up' and filed away – but nor can he be dismissed as irrelevant.

As his fellow Jews would have seen it, Jesus was claiming to be the long-awaited agent of deliverance. Yet he promised a kind of deliverance that seemed wrong to so much of his audience. Luke tells us that in his first sermon in the synagogue in Nazareth Jesus read the allotted passage of Scripture from Isaiah about the coming Messiah, then, having calmly rolled up the scroll, he said, 'Today this Scripture is fulfilled.' But there was no crashing intervention from God, coming to Israel's help, which was what many people had been expecting. Instead, Jesus went on with his quiet revolution.

We know from the circumstances of his death that Jesus was not just put to death by the Jewish authorities. Crucifixion was a Roman form of execution, and it is unlikely that the Romans would have executed a man such as Jesus simply because the Jewish leaders (under Roman control) had requested it. The Romans must have had their own reasons.

So the grounds for Jesus' condemnation were twofold. For many of his contemporaries, Jesus' words and actions constituted blasphemy against the Jewish Law. For the Romans, anxious to put down any revolt, Jesus' deeds could be interpreted as sedition against the occupying powers.

In any case, whatever interpretation we put on the evidence of the Gospel accounts, Jesus was going to die precisely because of those ideas which had made him notorious. He was to die because he challenged the prevailing notions of what people are and how they should behave.

He was to die because he challenged the prevailing notions of what people are and how they should behave.

As we know, however, there was one more notion to overturn.

THE CRUCIFIXION

Jesus' death was painful, slow and humiliating. Crucifixion was a fairly common form of death in those days, designed to be so horrible as a public warning, a deterrent to all who might threaten the peace of the realm. The same thinking lay behind the gibbet used in this country, right up to the Victorian period. The offender was not just killed, by a very public form of torture – the body was also physically degraded.

The significance of Jesus' death lies in the body. Who exactly was crucified? Was he divine? Again, we need to pause for a moment.

> *The offender was not just killed, by a very
> public form of torture – the body was
> also physically degraded.*

The claims made for Jesus after his death – that the man killed on the cross was also God – were unique. While it is true that there are many Greek and pagan myths of so-called 'god-men', what they portrayed was a totally foreign idea to Judaism. The first to proclaim Christ as Lord were Jews, and traditionally for them God was 'wholly other'. Judaism has no tradition of 'incarnation' – that is, of God or gods indwelling human beings or coming to earth in bodily form. It would not have been easy for the disciples to proclaim Jesus as the son of God. Not only was it foreign to their tradition to claim divinity in a human being, but that same human being had been publicly degraded and killed. After such a death, surely the disciples would not have claimed divinity for Jesus *unless* they believed it was true. Still less would they have made an even more shocking claim: his resurrection.

As your guide, I must tell you frankly that while we can be absolutely sure that Jesus lived, that he was a remarkable teacher who did amazing things, and that he was certainly crucified on the cross, we cannot with the same certainty say that we *know* he was raised by God from the dead.

Ah! I can almost see some journalists reaching for their pens: 'ARCHBISHOP DOUBTS THE RESURRECTION OF JESUS CHRIST' is an attractive headline!

Well, put your pens down.

I firmly believe that God raised Jesus from the dead, and I will offer you some thoughts about this in a moment. But proving that the resurrection happened is clearly much more difficult than proving that Jesus lived and died. Death happens to us all and is verifiable; the resurrection is clearly not of this order – indeed, it goes against human experience and our first instinct is incredulity.

> *Proving that the resurrection happened is clearly much more difficult than proving that Jesus lived and died.*

So why should anyone calmly conclude that Jesus actually rose from the grave?

The truth is, no one should. In his life and death, and most particularly in his resurrection, Jesus embodied that unexpected kingdom of God about which he taught – that overturning of human expectations. Just as Jesus overturned the tables of the corrupt money-changers in the temple, so he overturned all human expectations of life – and death. The resurrection of Christ is the conquering of death, the contradiction of the most definite fact in life. Who would accept that calmly?

Even if we must make our way to the resurrection by a leap of faith, by a willingness to accept the ways of God, there are some considerations that might help us.

THE EMPTY TOMB

All the Gospels make it clear that when the disciples went to embalm the body of Jesus it was missing. Of course, that proves nothing apart from the fact that a body went missing. It would have been the easiest thing in the world for the authorities to produce the body and so put down the rumours of a living Jesus. Perhaps they did not do this because they could not, and the body was really gone.

It would have been the easiest thing in the world for the authorities to produce the body and so put down the rumours of a living Jesus.

If we accept the fact of the empty tomb, as the evidence requires us to do, we are left with two possibilities. Either Jesus was resuscitated and helped from the tomb to appear among his disciples a few days later, convincing them that he was alive; or the same Jesus, crucified and truly dead, was triumphantly raised by his Father to lead all people into his kingdom. The first alternative is, I suggest, simply too implausible for words. To believe that a severely wounded man with torn hands and feet and a wound in his side could appear whole and well three days later is absurd. The second, the outrageous alternative – that the same Jesus who was crucified was raised from the tomb – is the firm conviction of the New Testament and the message of the Church.

JESUS' APPEARANCES TO HIS FOLLOWERS

This tradition also features in each of the Gospels. Of course, continuing our vein of scepticism, this too could have been fabricated by the first writers to prove the divinity of Jesus. But why should disciples who had fled the scene in such abject terror return a few days later and boldly say that they had met with Jesus and he was alive? It hardly seems credible – unless they actually *had* seen Jesus and were totally convinced that their Lord had conquered death.

Indeed, eye witnesses are central to the story – not only Peter and the first disciples, but also later people like Paul, whose testimony is one of the earliest written down. Paul talks of the risen Jesus appearing to him. Such is the sober, factual testimony of such witnesses that they convey a quiet, authoritative ring of truth.

Eye witnesses are central to the story.

Then something curious happens. As the tiny group of followers meet and begin to preach the resurrection of Jesus, so they change their 'holy day' from Saturday to Sunday, the day the resurrection took place. This is a clue of immense significance. Only something very dramatic and profound could have led devout Jews to do this, to openly go against a centuries-old tradition. We know what it was: the resurrection.

THE BIRTH OF THE CHURCH

Finally, and most convincingly, without the resurrection it is very difficult to explain the existence of the Church. The fact is that without the resurrection of Jesus there would be no Christianity, no Church and certainly no second millennium celebrations. The resurrection is the only reason the story of Jesus survives in the Gospel accounts. There is not a book in the New Testament which does not depend on its truth. It is the 'crux' of the matter. It formed the centre of the earliest preaching and it is the only thing that makes sense of the entire business.

There is one more thing I must say about the resurrection. It is not just an event back there in history: it continues to be an experience in the lives of the present-day followers of Jesus Christ who form his body, the Church.

DOES THE CHURCH DEMONSTRATE THAT EXPERIENCE OF RESURRECTION?

This is the question the Church must ask itself as it faces the end of one millennium and the start of another.

When I read the Gospels as a young man, I was surprised to discover that Jesus spent hardly any time at all in religious buildings. His first and celebrated sermon in the synagogue in Nazareth resulted in near disaster as he was evicted from it. His first recorded visit as an adult to the temple in Jerusalem ended with him nearly causing a riot by turning over the tables of the money-changers. He certainly was not a welcome visitor in religious buildings.

When I read the Gospels as a young man, I was surprised to discover that Jesus spent hardly any time at all in religious buildings.

I am reminded of Desmond Tutu's story of the small black boy during the apartheid era who had been cast out of an 'all-white' church. As he wept on the church steps with the church door firmly closed behind him, the Lord appeared dressed in white and, sitting down with the boy, said gently, 'Don't worry, my boy. I've been trying to get into that church for years!' Desmond's point was that organized religion and Jesus do not always mix happily.

Organized religion and Jesus do not always mix happily.

This was clearly so in Jesus' time. After that incident in Nazareth, he seemed to spend most of his time speaking to people in the open air; and having heard his arresting teaching, people started to follow him. It is not an exaggeration to speak of a 'Jesus movement' as the people crowded around him. They listened eagerly to his teaching, were impressed by his authority and sought his healing.

From this motley group of men and women, the later Church has become a body of nearly 2 billion people who claim, in some shape or form, to be believers and followers of this person Jesus today. While it has to be said that the Church in the West has been shrinking during the last century, this is not the whole story. In many parts of the world the Church is thriving. It includes a bigger proportion of the world's population than it has ever done before. Right around the globe there are growing churches that far outstrip in terms of numbers anything that Western Europe has experienced this century.

Without apology, I want to say that I am proud of the universal Church and the particular branch I represent. This body continues to be a powerful force for good in the world.

THE CHURCH IS NOT PERFECT

Nevertheless, as the third millennium begins it is important to acknowledge that many awful things have been done in the name of the Church which blight the good name of the Founder of Christianity.

At times in its history, the Church has defamed the name of Jesus Christ. It played a part in the Crusades, of course, and in the victimization of Jews in the Middle Ages and in Nazi Germany, the Conquistador invasions of South America, and the 'wars of religion' at the time of the Reformation. It has contributed to the oppression of women; to policies of imperialism, slavery, and the repression of free speech; and in so many situations, sadly, it has proved a stumbling block to the establishment of a just or lasting peace. All these examples – a mere selection – demonstrate the terrible way in which we have let Jesus Christ down.

The Church, like its constituent members, can never be more than human. In spite of our calling to be people who exemplify a gospel of freedom and peace, and the many magnificent examples of those who have practised that, history shows that we have fallen a long way short of these high standards. But however much we may dislike the inadequacies of such a body, and disown its terrible history, the power of Jesus Christ in his body can empower its renewal. Of course, there are those who on principle would say with the nineteenth-century writer George Tyrell that, 'I would welcome Jesus Christ if he did not come with his leprous bride, the Church.' Colourfully put! But that's just the problem with Jesus: he turns up in the most curious company and sees possibilities of redemption everywhere.

That's just the problem with Jesus: he turns up in the most curious company and sees possibilities of redemption everywhere.

Just as Christ lived alongside us, recognized our humanity and sought to inspire us to transcend it, should we not work continually to improve the Church?

The question all churches must address is this: *How can we once again become a powerful tool of God's kingdom?* In other words, how can we call all people to the loving claims of a God who is 'Our Father'?

We know the answer already. The Church's duty is to embody Jesus for the world – to seek to *be* him. Based on the portrait we have discovered of Jesus so far, what does that mean the Church should be?

The essence of Jesus, as I see him, is *self-giving*. This is not the same as self-sacrifice – that implies, to modern ears, an unhealthy negation of one's own personality. Self-giving is a far more costly thing. Instead of simply 'doing away' with our own desires and feelings, if we wish to be self-giving we must *redirect* them towards the service of others. A self-giving Church is one which, regardless of the cost to itself, will be absolutely dedicated to the needs of others. It will not wilfully throw away its long-standing and hallowed traditions to do this. But it will be prepared to put itself on the line, as Jesus did.

We must remind ourselves that our sole reason for existence is to celebrate the gift of his life, and to serve the world in which we live. That will require radical adjustment to the way we live and behave. Just as Jesus surprised people with his unorthodox ideas of what the Messiah or the Law should mean, the Church must surprise people who expect all institutions to be the same. We must reject insularity, exclusion and the assertions of petty power. Most of all, we must look with Jesus towards a new world, almost within our grasp, where the corrupt order of this present world is changed for ever.

The Church must surprise people who expect all institutions to be the same.

The Church should be working with dedication and conviction to bring about a new age – the kingdom of God.

Some will ask: *Is the kingdom of God relevant to the journey we are making to the future signified by the new millennium?*

The transition to the next millennium is not like crossing a border on holiday, with the barrier smoothly rising to the vertical, like a clock's hands at midnight. We will not immediately find ourselves in a new country, or a new world. We are on a journey to discover an unknown region. In one sense it is not a totally *new* journey, because we know the human race has not made a complete success of any period of time we have passed through so far.

The twentieth century has seen the human race reach an unprecedented level of sophistication, but it has also been a century of unprecedented violence and greed, leading to unimaginable destruction. Even as we leave the 'old world' behind us, we carry in our baggage the means to complete the destruction not only of our species, but also of the precious planet on which our species depends. This is a crucial journey for us, then, full of fears and responsibilities.

We carry in our baggage the means to complete the destruction not only of our species, but also of the precious planet on which our species depends.

Yet we can make that journey with tranquillity and trust – if we take with us certain elements from the story of the life, death and resurrection of Jesus. I call them *identity*, *direction* and *hope*.

IDENTITY

Essential for any journey is a sense of identity. We must know who we are and where we come from. Few great explorers have completed their quest suffering from amnesia! Being is not enough for us humans: we also need to belong.

One of the most significant European thinkers of our day, Vaclav Havel, has written:

> *I believe with the loss of God, man has lost a kind of absolute and universal system of co-ordinates, to which he could always relate anything, chiefly himself. His world and his personality gradually begin to break up into separate, incoherent fragments to different, relative co-ordinates. And when this has happened, man begins to lose his inner identity, that is, his identity with himself.*

This is not just a description of modern humankind. Jesus also recognized that lack of secure identity in the audience he addressed. In fact, he would not be surprised to find it still being commented on today. For him, it was a natural part of the human condition. He described the people he saw all those years ago as 'people without a shepherd', 'prodigal' sons and daughters wandering far from home, like people searching for the 'pearl of great price' and unable to find meaning for their lives.

His audience were the same as today, good people doing the best they could with what they had. Yet his message assumed that there is in all of us a feeling that we are not who we *should* be: that we are, in some way, lost. He saw how, without the knowledge of God, we can feel separated from all that surrounds us. This is the cry of much modern music and film drama. We feel separated from ourselves, from others and from God. As we stand at the close of one millennium and the dawn of another, this is the search for identity that Jesus can truly fulfil.

Jesus offered an eternal solution to the guilt and shame of our many mistakes; a way of setting straight our disjointed lives. To give of yourself in love, as Jesus showed in his life and words – and continues to show to Christians today – is to discover your true, complete identity. Jesus' message is eternally relevant: '*I have come that you might have life and have it in abundance.*' Perhaps, then, Jesus shows us both who we are and who we should be. Millions of people over the last 2,000 years – and millions still today – testify that through Jesus forgiveness and a new sense of belonging in God's family are made available. Certainly the West needs to rediscover this. The Chief Rabbi of Great Britain, Dr Jonathan Sacks, wrote a few years ago: 'Secularization has failed to provide us with our most basic human needs, the need for meaning and personal identity.'

Jesus offered an eternal solution to the guilt and shame of our many mistakes; a way of setting straight our disjointed lives.

DIRECTION

Along with this sense of identity, we must also cultivate a sense of direction, if our journey to the future is ever to succeed. If our sense of identity comes from knowing ourselves, then our sense of direction comes from knowing God.

WHAT IS GOD LIKE?

We have seen how central the Lord's Prayer was in the teaching of Jesus. *What is God like?* we sometimes ask. The Christian faith replies: *Look at Jesus.* The Gospel of John proclaims that Jesus said, 'To see me is to see the Father.' It was an extraordinary statement and, as his opponents saw it, it was an offensive statement at the same time. But it is one from which Christians cannot shrink, because it is the way we see God: as someone who loves us, who cares for us and who is like us in every way except for the question of sin. As I see Jesus and read his message for our times, I see him pointing the way to the Father.

The kind of future we will move into requires an acknowledgement of God. The terrible abuses perpetrated on the world by 'Christians' have already been described – but this century has seen even greater crimes coming from those who acknowledge no God at all. We may think, in the West, that the days of such tyrants and dictators are over. But even we, for all our sophistication, have no certainty in that. Without God, and even without the idolatrous ideologies which have poisoned this century, many people sense an ominous lack of direction. And well they might, if the nearest thing to a Supreme Being that the 'developed' world can acknowledge is the 'Market', or 'Economic Forces'. Surely, if we wish to enter a new world in the year 2000, we must turn afresh to God.

We may think that the days of tyrants and dictators are over. But even we, for all our sophistication, have no certainty in that.

HOPE

With Jesus' help, therefore, we can know who we are and where we should be going. But there is a final ingredient we need: hope.

Heaven is not just 'pie in the sky when I die'.

We have seen that his message was 'the kingdom'. For Jesus the kingdom was first and foremost the rule of God in the hearts and lives of us all. That kingdom, that heaven, is not just 'pie in the sky when I die'. It is not some kind of divine aspirin to get us through the daily grind of life on earth. Eternal life does not simply await us when we die: it starts right now in a relationship with God, through Jesus Christ, which continues for ever. It begins when a person starts on the journey with God and moves towards him. We do not have to know all the answers to start; we only need the willingness and humility to begin.

We do not have to know all the answers to start; we only need the willingness and humility to begin.

To be honest, it is hard to start. Perhaps that is why Jesus himself likened the quest to children whose innocent, trusting attitude is the right model for discovering the nature of the kingdom. He said, 'Whoever does not welcome the kingdom of God like a little child will never enter it.' These are sobering words for 'sophisticated' people like me and you. It is not that the Christian faith is childish or shallow. Many great scientists and many of the best minds in the world follow Jesus today. Yet the truth about Jesus is so easy to grasp that even a child can reach out and accept it.

It is in that same spirit that we must go on into the next millennium. Unless we hope for a better world, how can we achieve one?

These three gifts from Jesus, *identity*, *direction* and *hope*, are to be treasured.

I have kept them in my mind since I started my own 'journey' over 40 years ago. And I can honestly say that maintaining a sense of all three is a challenge which still satisfies and thrills me. The person of Jesus Christ is the centre of my existence and he is the person I am growing towards in my personal living. I have seen countless others make this journey and their story, too, is that Jesus Christ offers life and hope and peace.

> *The person of Jesus Christ is the centre of my existence and he is the person I am growing towards in my personal living.*

Mind you, he offers many challenges as well. He offers much and demands much. That is 'life in abundance'. As one of my predecessors as Archbishop of Canterbury once said of the Christian life, 'The entry fee is nothing but the annual subscription is everything.' We cannot play around with being a Christian. It has serious implications for the way we live and behave.

For all of us there is still the question which pursues us down 2,000 years of time, the question which Jesus put to his first disciples: '*Who do you say I am?*' Peter, you will remember, answered by saying, 'You are the Christ, the Son of God.' That answer changed his life and gave him a purpose for living.

> *The future has no terrors if we know the person*
> *who holds the key to the future.*

There are no easy promises, no glib assurances and no quick fixes – just the presence of Jesus wherever we are and whoever we are. The future has no terrors if we know the person who holds the key to the future.

> *May God bless you on your millennium journey.*

+ George Carey

FOR FURTHER REFLECTION

During the millennium celebrations, I encourage you to spend some time on your own thinking about Jesus and the year 2000. Take time, perhaps, to read for yourself the Lord's Prayer on page 18 of this book. Reach out to God and ask him to speak to you.

Try to get hold of a modern translation of the Bible, available in almost every bookshop, and read about the life of Jesus in the Gospel accounts by Matthew, Mark, Luke or John.

Find time to visit a church during the year 2000. It may take more than one visit to find one that is relevant to you. But keep going, and look for a place that is welcoming and that gives you the space to reflect on the meaning behind the millennium.